T0208696

THE
BIBLE
IS GREAT!

DAMIAN GEMMA

WESTBOW
PRESS®
A DIVISION OF THOMAS NELSON
& ZONDERVAN

WestBow Press books may be ordered through booksellers or by contacting:

WestBow Press
A Division of Thomas Nelson & Zondervan
1663 Liberty Drive
Bloomington, IN 47403
www.westbowpress.com
1 (866) 928-1240

ISBN: 978-1-9736-4966-3 (sc)
ISBN: 978-1-9736-4965-6 (e)

Library of Congress Control Number: 2018914946

Print information available on the last page.

WestBow Press rev. date: 1/14/2019

CONTENTS

INTRODUCTION

The Bible is Great! That may indeed be the biggest understatement of all time. It is truly a divine miracle right from God and His ultimate "love note" to each and every one of us. His love for us is simply amazing and so completely thorough. It is agape love. This book focuses specifically on two Old Testament verses; Psalm 22 and Isaiah 53 respectively. There are many other prophetic verses as well. The book highlights the incredible journey the Bible has taken. The compelling prophesy of the Messiah and His (Jesus) sacrifice for all sin for all time forever and ever. Tetelestai (It is finished). So, take a ride on route 66 it is one you will clearly need and enjoy as you come to the realization that the Bible is integral to the condition of your soul. God has gone to incredible lengths to save you, even to the point of the cross. That is how much He loves us. Thanks be to our incredible Lord. He has saved us for eternity and infinity. Can you comprehend infinity?

Biblical history is indeed incredible. Is it history or should it simply be called His Story? After reading this, I'm hoping you will conclude that the Bible is great!

Dedication

First and foremost, this book is dedicated to our Lord and Savior, Jesus Christ. He is and always will be our very best friend.

This book is also dedicated to the memories of Joseph Vincent Gemma and Betty Jane Gemma for always teaching us about faith in Christ Jesus and always loving us so very much.

Lastly this is dedicated to my siblings Lisa, Adrienne, Dino and Lisa G. I thank them so very much for their kindness, love and support.

Chapter 1

Time Element BC and AD

Let us first define the denotations of time. BC means Before the Birth of Christ. AD stands for Anno Domini which is Latin for "in the year of our Lord." Again, based entirely on His birth, some people think it means after death which it clearly does not. We are 2,018 years after the birth of Christ. Jesus lived 33 years. So, we are 1,985 years after His death and 2,018 years after His birth. So that is where your time context is defined. Contemplate that our entire system of time is based on the life of a poor Jewish carpenter. Time is defined by the life of Jesus, based on His birth in a small town named Bethlehem (The City of David).

Try to understand this even from just a purely historical, chronological, conceptual, genealogical and/or factual perspective. One does not even necessarily need to view the concept of time from a religious perspective in order to understand the context of all of this. Make the PARELLEL yourself.

Try to consider that the most famous person in all of history is a poor Jewish carpenter. That is right. Jesus Christ is the most famous person in all of history. Who else's life changed both history and time? It is a certainty. There is no way around it. God gives us all of the answers to all of the questions throughout the Bible. We just have to become better evaluators. Why are we so dense? Our entire system of time is based on the life of Jesus. What year are you in? 2018 represents 2,018 years after the birth of Jesus Christ. AD does not mean after death like some people believe but rather it means Anno Domini which is Latin for in the year of our Lord. So, our entire time system is based on His birth and His life. Religious or not, you have to try to grasp the fact that God came as a man and in doing so He changed the world and time as we know it. He loves us so much that even in our doubt and weakness of faith He alone provides all of the answers. He is the answer for yesterday, today and tomorrow. Wow we have an incredible God. Whether we are able to see it and comprehend it really is up to us. I am a believer and that is easy to see, but I would argue that based on the factual information, archaeology, history and Bible prophesy that it is much more difficult to be a non-believer. History is a compilation of events that have occurred, and these events show us where we have come from, where we are currently, and where we are going. This life is the temporal one. So, examine the history and try to explain how a poor Jewish carpenter can change time forever, and how He is manifested in our lives. I pray each and every person would see it and recognize it. In this case, the only way we are going to see it and recognize it, is by the pure grace of God. Everything Jesus says will happen, happens just as He says it will be including His death and His resurrection. He tells us that His words will never pass away, and they never do. God does everything for a reason; His reason. Read the Bible and try to live it!

This is a map for our life, an instruction manual if you will. The messages that exist in the Bible are ones that I believe are directly from God and in fact exemplify the kind of person that God wants us to strive to be. We certainly have the very best teacher in Jesus. He shows us by His love. It is a blessing among blessings that we have the Bible.

> **Romans 15:4 For whatever things were written before were written for our learning, that we through the patience and comfort of the Scriptures might have hope.**

CHAPTER 2

Eloi, Eloi, Lama Sabanthani

My God, My God, why have you forsaken Me? These are the words spoken by Jesus from the cross. God is everything that matters in our lives. He is the important part so following Him should always be the path we follow, always trying to emulate the incredible example Jesus has set for each of us. He is completely awesome. His love truly has no bounds. It really doesn't. It is magnificent. He is King and ruler over all that exists. The world belongs to Him and He will come back to claim it. We serve an incredible God who absolutely adores us. Do not let the world tell you otherwise. We need to keep humble and love and admire the greatness of God. He alone is all powerful. He will not fit in our human box, not now and not ever. He is the Lord. He has dominion over all things and He provides so abundantly. We are His flock for now and for always.

God the Father has placed all sin for all time on His Son Jesus. The sacrifice Jesus makes covers all sin forever and ever. It has to be done this way. Jesus is the sacrificial Lamb. We have all been bought and paid for at a great price. Thanks be to our most holy and loving God. He is truly awesome. Jesus' last words from the cross are Tetelestai (It is finished). He has done it and we are indeed saved by His blood. He is the perfect Lamb. This is how much God loves each and every one of us.

> **Psalm 22:1 (Old Testament) My God, My God why have You forsaken Me? Why are you so far from helping Me? And from the words of my groaning?**

> **Matthew 27::46 (New Testament)**

> **About three in the afternoon Jesus cried out in a loud voice, "Eloi, Eloi, Lama Sabachthani?" (which means "My God, my God, why have you forsaken me?").**

CHAPTER 3

Bible Journey

The Bible has been banned and burned. It has been outlawed, banished, refuted, disrespected, disputed, debated, desecrated, questioned and ridiculed. It has been taken out of our schools and in many cases, it has been deemed as inappropriate and politically incorrect. Scotland alone made it completely illegal to even possess, own, lend or quote a Bible for well over 150 years. (early 1400's to mid 1500's). Somehow the Bible made it through the violent Crusades and other religious wars. Still, the Bible has withstood it all, and it is still right with us just like always. It will always be with us. Just like our Lord, it is always there, and just like our Lord, it gives us hope. Today's world needs the Bible and its teachings probably more than any other time in the history of the world. The world is so very, very lost. Just look around or turn on the news. The Bible shows us how God wants us to treat each other. The good book's greatest message is to love one another. It is the greatest teaching tool of all time, and Jesus is in fact the greatest teacher of all time. You and I will be long gone and forgotten, and they will still be reading the Bible. They will still be talking about Jesus. They always will. Jesus tells us that "My words will never fade away." They never do. The Bible has been translated more than any other book in the history of the world. From Hebrew to Aramaic to Greek to Latin to English to Spanish. It has lasted generation after generation. There are many versions of the Bible. It does not claim to be a science, history or medical book, yet all of the science, history and medicine in the Bible has been proven to be absolutely true. Biblical prophecy is downright amazing. You will find the ultimate encouragement throughout God's word ... The Bible. What an incredible message and what an incredible love. It is a journey that you will both need and enjoy. It is a journey you will indeed love. It is the greatest journey of all. There is nothing greater than God's word. Absolutely NOTHING GREATER ......

> 2nd Timothy 3:16 (New Testament) All is given by inspiration of God and is profitable for doctrine, for reproof, for correction, for instruction in righteousness, that the man of God may be complete, thoroughly equipped for every good work.

CHAPTER 4

The Septuagint (Greek)

You have probably heard the phrase, "It's all Greek to me." The *Septuagint* is the Greek translation of the Hebrew bible. This happened between 250 B.C. and 200 B.C. It is labeled as an extant copy. Extant means existing, current, and text that stands out. It (*The Septuagint*) was compiled in Alexandria, Egypt which was founded in 332 B.C. The Hebrew bible was translated by 70 Jewish Scholars, Scribes, and Elders. In actuality, there were 72 translators. The Hebrew bible, also called the Torah, represents the beginning of the Septuagint. Each of the translators was told to translate the text identically. The text itself represents Masoretic themes throughout the Septuagint. The last chapter of the old testament was completed and translated in 132 B.C. Additionally, new testament scripture was translated from 200 A.D. to 370 A.D.

Most words in the English language have a Greek origin. For instance, if you look at the word psalms it comes from the Greek word psalmos which means the strumming or playing of instrumental music. It even sounds like songs.

The Septuagint is once again an example of the Bible being translated. It is indeed the most translated book throughout all history.

As far as we know, the Bible was written in Hebrew and then later transcribed into Greek, Aramaic, Latin and later into English and Spanish. It has survived wars and War Lords, burning and banishment and even slander, insult and ridicule. It is still here and always will be.

The history of the Bible is very compelling. Many have tried unsuccessfully to destroy it. Here is the thing though: it cannot and will not be destroyed. Scotland made it illegal to even have or own a Bible. Other countries have also tried to put an end to the good book, but they have also been unsuccessful. Like our Jesus, the Bible lives on. It is a crystal-clear message of LOVE.

Psalm 22 and Isiah 53 are represented in both *The Dead Sea Scrolls and The Septuagint*. Bible prophecy is evident throughout *The Septuagint*. God's word is really amazing.

Ephesians 4:19 To know the love of Christ which passes knowledge; that you may be filled with all the fullness of God.

CHAPTER 5

The Dead Sea Scrolls

The Dead Sea Scrolls are also a large component in Bible history and archaeology. They are found near the city of Qumran, close to the west bank of Israel. The caves themselves are located proximate to the Dead Sea. *The Dead Sea Scrolls* were written approximately between 161 B.C. and 73 A.D. All of the books in the Old Testament are included except Esther and Nehemiah. So, 37 of the 39 Old Testament books are included in *The Dead Sea Scrolls*.

The scrolls were discovered in 1947 by a Bedoin shepherd. For the first 15 years, until 1962, the scrolls consist of mainly 255 pages of artifacts. Between 1962 and 1977, a 15 year period, continued restoration of the caves produces another 800 documents. They have been carbon dated and carbon tested for their accuracy. Further restoration of the 11 caves and countless excavations produced the completed scrolls.

After another 15 years in 1992, technology found The Dead Sea Scrolls. Archaeologists use imaging and digitization and all of the current methods to date and authenticate The Dead Sea Scrolls.

The Scrolls have had a profound effect on scholarship, the Hebrew Bible, second temple Judaism, and early Christianity.

The paragraph listed below is attributed to www. bl.uk:

"These celebrated texts are of unique historical and religious significance. More than 800 manuscripts, written on papyrus or animal skin, were discovered in caves by the Dead Sea only 50 years ago. They include virtually the only known surviving Biblical documents written before the second century."

Conclusively, one can say that The Dead Sea Scrolls are vital to the continuous manifestation of the obvious prophecy and history of the greatest book ever written, The Bible.

> **Jeremiah 23:29 "Is not My word like a fire?" says the Lord, "And like a hammer that breaks the rock in pieces."**

CHAPTER 6

The Torah

The books of the Torah were given to Moses at Mount Sinai in 1312 B.C. by God. Torah itself is Hebrew, and means instruction, teaching, or law. It is also known as the Pentateuch. The first five books of the Bible include Genesis, Exodus, Leviticus, Numbers, and Deuteronomy. All of these books are labeled as the books of Moses. This is of utmost importance when examining a historic context of the Bible. While they are considered the books of Moses, the translation takes place over a period of 170 years. Each book is also attributed to several Judean scribes. The very first name given to our God almighty is Elohim. In Genesis 2, God's name becomes Yahweh. Later, He is referred to as Jehovah. Now, we simply call Him God.

There are basically two types of Torah. The first being the written Torah, the second being the verbal Torah. The very first oration came from God himself, spoken to Moses. This results in two types of followers of The Torah. The first being the Eloists which is the oldest, the second being the Jahwist. The Jahwist is an example of later texts of The Torah. The Torah is translated into 70 different languages. Of these, the most popular translation is the one from Hebrew into English. It is also known as the Chumash. It has a general connotation once again to the first five books of the Hebrew Bible. The Torah is not the first reference but is one of the first references to the Godhead. We indeed have a plural God, the Father (Abba), the son (Jesus) and the Holy Spirit, (The Helper).

The text below is attributed to Wikipedia.org.

According to classical rabbinic texts this parallel set of material was originally transmitted to Moses at Sinai, and then from Moses to the people of Israel. At that time, it was forbidden to write and publish the oral law, as any writing would be incomplete and subject to misinterpretation and abuse.

The resources for The Bible are incredibly prophetic. If you examine the text closely, the Hebrew translation becomes the living Bible. One must come to the realization that if indeed these texts are in their original condition in a museum in Israel, then the archaeology is both true and compelling. Finally, the translations are more than evident that we indeed have a Hebrew God, a Hebrew Messiah, and a Hebrew Torah, which all become a vital part of our sanctification.

> **Psalm 119:2 "Blessed are those who keep His testimonies, who seek Him with the whole heart!**

CHAPTER 7

The Quran (Muslim/Islamic)

The Muslim/Islamic bible is known as the Quran. There are 114 chapters in the totality of the Quran. It was completed in the year 632 A.D. In the Quran God is referred to as Allah. The capital is called Mecca. The prophet Muhammad is said to have been guided by the messaging angel, Gabriel. The Quran is written and transcribed in Arabic language. In the Muslim faith, one would attend a Mosque. Muhammad is referred to as unlettered, which means he could not read or write.

A real Muslim is a complete pacifist. This means that they believe in absolutely no violence whatsoever. The correlation to the holy Hebrew Bible is well known. There are over 100 existing references to Jesus Christ, another 100 references to Moses, and an additional 25 references to Mother Mary. Contrarily, the prophet Muhammad is referenced in The Quran only two times. The writing of the Quran takes place in more than a 20 year period from 610 A.D. through 632 A.D. In that same year, 632 A. D. Muhammad (peace be upon him) died at the age of 60.

It is imperative to understand that the history of the Quran is merely less than 1500 years as compared to the Hebrew Bible which is several thousand years. No additional artifacts or archaeology have been found, and there are none that suggest any earlier date. Both the Hebrew Bible and the Muslim Quran are indeed references to a most holy God. Both books acknowledge the existence of God. The gentle nature of God is expressed in both of these books. The unending grace of God is also expressed in both of these books. Additionally, both books are written and authored for a general audience. Both of these books exemplify a desire for peace. The only difference is that the Quran acknowledges Jesus Christ as a great teacher. The Hebrew Bible, of course, acknowledges Jesus Christ as the Messiah.

> **Acts 20:24 But none of these things move me; nor do I count my life dear to myself, so that I may finish my race with joy and the ministry which I received from The Lord Jesus, to testify to the gospel of the grace of God.**

CHAPTER 8

Crucifixion

Let us examine crucifixion and its history. The very first crucifixion takes place in Greece in 479 BC (5th century BC). The Athenians were the first to practice this horrific torture process for capital punishment crimes and executions. Crucifixion was next used by the Phoenicians from approximately 450 BC to 150 BC. (300 years). It was introduced in Rome in 150 BC. The Romans perfected this vicious, torturous, sadistic and violent execution process. They employed crucifixion and even developed methods utilized in the process to the extent that it became extremely difficult for the person being crucified to even breathe. The victim would ultimately die from asphyxiation. Rome utilized this cruel torture technique for more than 500 years. Finally, the emperor Constantine abolished crucifixion in the late 300's (4th century AD). So, from strictly and simply a historical and contextual perspective, crucifixion is not even invented or utilized until 479 BC. Crucifixion lasts roughly 900 years. Psalm 22 and Isiah 53 are written far before crucifixion is ever invented.

It is more than obvious that both Psalm 22 and Isiah 53 are written and authored long before the invention of crucifixion. In the case of psalms, crucifixion is not utilized or recognized for more than 400 years. When King David wrote the psalms, crucifixion is not invented. Jesus is not even born for at least 880 years after Psalm 22. In addition, Psalm 22 was written at least 400 years before the invention of crucifixion.

In the case of Isiah 53, once again, if you examine both the timeline and the context, you will clearly see Jesus is not born, and crucifixion is not invented. In the case of Isiah 53, it is written and authored at least 200 years before crucifixion and nearly 700 years before the time of Jesus.

Crucifixion was devised to not only be extremely excruciating, but also indeed humiliating. The violent methods often included nailing the hands and feet to a wooden cross, and hanging the victim for several hours, if not days, until their ultimate demise would take place. This is what your savior has done for you. He loves you.

In Luke chapter 23

Then Jesus said, "Father, forgive them, for they do not know what they do."

And they divided His garments and cast lots.

This is the divine nature of God. Jesus was being crucified by them. Yet, Jesus was praying for their forgiveness.

One of the Pharisees walked by the cross of Jesus. Jesus had his eyes closed and his head down but is speaking softly. The Pharisee asked the Roman guard "What is he saying?" The guard answers, "He is praying for you." This is the kind of savior that all of us have in Jesus Christ.

The following is taken from biblestudytools.com

Then the governor's soldiers took Jesus into the Praetorium and gathered the whole company of soldiers around him.

They stripped him and put a scarlet robe on him,

and then twisted together a crown of thorns and set it on his head. They put a staff in his right hand. Then they knelt in front of him and mocked him. "Hail, king of the Jews!" they said.

They spit on him and took the staff and struck him on the head again and again.

After they had mocked him, they took off the robe and put his own clothes on him. Then they led him away to crucify him.

As they were going out, they met a man from Cyrene, named Simon, and they forced him to carry the cross.

They came to a place called Golgotha (which means "the place of the skull").

There they offered Jesus wine to drink, mixed with gall; but after tasting it, he refused to drink it.

When they had crucified him, they divided up his clothes by casting lots.

And sitting down, they kept watch over him there.

Above his head they placed the written charge against him: THIS IS JESUS, THE KING OF THE JEWS.

Two rebels were crucified with him, one on his right and one on his left.

Those who passed by hurled insults at him, shaking their heads and saying, "You who are going to destroy the temple and build it in three days, save yourself! Come down from the cross, if you are the Son of God!"

In the same way the chief priests, the teachers of the law and the elders mocked him.

"He saved others," they said, "but he can't save himself! He's the king of Israel! Let him come down now from the cross, and we will believe in him.

He trusts in God. Let God rescue him now if he wants him, for he said, 'I am the Son of God.'

In the same way the rebels who were crucified with him also heaped insults on him.

From noon until three in the afternoon darkness came over all the land.

About three in the afternoon Jesus cried out in a loud voice, "Eli, Eli, lemasabachthani?" (which means "My God, my God, why have you forsaken me?").

When some of those standing there heard this, they said, "He's calling Elijah."

Immediately one of them ran and got a sponge. He filled it with wine vinegar, put it on a staff, and offered it to Jesus to drink.

The rest said, "Now leave him alone. Let's see if Elijah comes to save him."

And when Jesus had cried out again in a loud voice, he gave up his spirit.

Mathew 27:54 When the centurion and those with him who were guarding Jesus saw the earthquake and all that had happened, they were terrified, and said, "Surely he was the Son of God!"

CHAPTER 9

Psalm 22 and Isiah 53

There are many verses and chapters in the Hebrew bible which depict and describe the Messiah and His ultimate sacrifice. Sacrifice itself is present throughout the Bible. Back in the book of Exodus, for the very first Passover, the Hebrews were instructed to take the blood of a perfect lamb and place it on the top, the sides, and the base of the door so the angel of death would pass them over. This signifies a cross and would be prophetic in predicting the sacrifice of the Christ. There are many other verses and chapters which are prophetic in predicting the Messiah, however, these two seem to stand out significantly.

It is perhaps the very most important of all of the Psalms. The twenty second Psalm ... Do you understand it? ... Can you understand it? What it means... the significance ... it's relevance... the significance of the context? Why it is so important? The importance of the timing and the prophesy. Psalm 22 was written about 900 years before Jesus is even born. It is written more than 400 years before crucifixion is even invented. It is so clearly vital. It is vital to our faith. It is vital to our very being. Why is Psalm 22 so very essential to our faith? We must understand what it says, the content, how it is fulfilled and the context of when it is written. To realize that at the time in history that it is authored, crucifixion had not even yet been invented. Not until 479 BC. Not even invented, yet the details are clearly describing and depicting what would later be known as crucifixion. Can you grasp and comprehend that the crucifixion of Jesus occurred 900 years After Psalm 22 is even written?! The prophesy, predictions and the pre-destination could not be more evident. Consider 900 years before Christ's crucifixion. God's love for us is so enormous and so incredible. He allowed Himself to be the ultimate sacrifice, the ultimate provision, and only He is the complete, final and ultimate answer for our sin. Tetelestai, it is finished. We cannot save ourselves. God wanted His family back. We need to understand the willingness of God to subject Himself even to the point of the cross. He loves us that much and provides the Messiah through Jesus. The explicit details that are described are not some kind of coincidence. God did everything on purpose and for a reason ... His reason and His purpose. Everything.

In John 17, Jesus is praying. He says to God, You love them as much as You love Me.

What? God loves us the way He loves Jesus? It is just plain awesome. We are His children. His love is evident by His willingness to be our sacrifice. He has paid the way, and He has paved the way. We are each bought and paid for at a great price.

Be blessed with the knowledge that He loves us that much. It is indeed amazing grace; a grace that we clearly do not deserve. Psalm 22 depicts that ultimate grace and foretells the future crucifixion.

It is magnificent to think about the fact that Psalm 22 is quoted seven times in the New Testament, and each and every time in reference to Jesus Christ. Crucifixion was not known to King David. Crucifixion is still 400 years away.

Crucifixion did not exist in King David's culture; yet he

described it with such specificity that it is as accurate as the Gospel. How did David know that? Well, for instance, in Acts 2:30 the Holy Spirit says, "David was a prophet." In actuality, King David was a prophet.

So, we are given another example from the Holy Spirit of a future that has not yet occurred. The description is so accurate that we feel much like we were actually there, gathered around the Cross with the crowd watching as Jesus was crucified.

The Psalm has two parts. The first 21 verses are prayer. From verse 22 to 31 is praise. Prayer and praise. Certainly, a prophetic combination.

Psalm 22:

My God, My God, why have You forsaken Me?
Why are You so far from helping Me,
And from the words of My groaning?
O My God, I cry in the daytime, but You do not hear;
And in the night season, and am not silent.

But You *are* holy,
Enthroned in the praises of Israel.
Our fathers trusted in You;
They trusted, and You delivered them.
They cried to You, and were delivered;
They trusted in You, and were not ashamed.
But I *am* a worm, and no man;
A reproach of men, and despised by the people.
All those who see Me ridicule Me;
They shoot out the lip, they shake the head, *saying,*
"He trusted in the Lord, let Him rescue Him;
Let Him deliver Him, since He delights in Him!"

But You *are* He who took Me out of the womb;
You made Me trust *while* on My mother's breasts.
I was cast upon You from birth.
From My mother's womb
You *have been* My God.
Be not far from Me,
For trouble *is* near;
For *there is* none to help.

Many bulls have surrounded Me;
Strong *bulls* of Bashan have encircled Me.
They gape at Me *with* their mouths,
Like a raging and roaring lion.

1I am poured out like water,
And all My bones are out of joint;
My heart is like wax;
It has melted within Me.
My strength is dried up like a potsherd,
And My tongue clings to My jaws;
You have brought Me to the dust of death.

For dogs have surrounded Me;
The congregation of the wicked has enclosed Me.
They pierce My hands and My feet;
I can count all My bones.
They look *and* stare at Me.
They divide My garments among them,
And for My clothing they cast lots.

But You, O Lord, do not be far from Me;
O My Strength, hasten to help Me!
Deliver Me from the sword,

My precious *life* from the power of the dog.
Save Me from the lion's mouth
And from the horns of the wild oxen!

You have answered Me.

I will declare Your name to My brethren;
In the midst of the assembly I will praise You.
You who fear the Lord, praise Him!
All you descendants of Jacob, glorify Him,
And fear Him, all you offspring of Israel!
For He has not despised nor abhorred the affliction of the afflicted;
Nor has He hidden His face from Him;
But when He cried to Him, He heard.

My praise *shall be* of You in the great assembly;
I will pay My vows before those who fear Him.
The poor shall eat and be satisfied;
Those who seek Him will praise the Lord.
Let your heart live forever!

All the ends of the world
Shall remember and turn to the Lord,
And all the families of the nations
Shall worship before You.
For the kingdom *is* the Lord's,
And He rules over the nations.

All the prosperous of the earth
Shall eat and worship;
All those who go down to the dust

Shall bow before Him,
Even he who cannot keep himself alive.

A posterity shall serve Him.
It will be recounted of the Lord to the *next* generation,
They will come and declare His righteousness to a people who
will be born,
That He has done *this*.

> *Psalm 22:1 (Old Testament) My God, My God why
> have You forsaken Me? Why are you so far from
> helping Me? And from the words of my groaning?*

Now, let us examine the biblical as well as the historical
prophesy. Specifically, Isaiah 53 and the reference to the Savior.
The prophet, Isaiah, writes his Book of Isaiah roughly 700
years before the birth of Christ. Keep in mind once again, that
crucifixion has not yet been invented. It is possible that it was
an even longer time considering Isiah's lifespan was 60 years.
(740 BC to 681 BC). The book by Isaiah is and has been very well
documented and researched. It is included in both the Dead Sea
Scrolls and the Septuagint. The book is acknowledged as being
authored centuries before these scrolls but included in them.
Are you with me so far? .... Good. So, Isaiah is a prophet and
he foretells the future. He is so accurate and on the mark that
it eventually leads to his very own demise. Many became very
scared and afraid of his prophesy, predictions and foretelling.
Fear of the unknown. They end up sawing him in half at the
waist. Ouch!! I want to highlight some of the words used in this
prophetic writing. So here goes:

Despised, Rejected, Stricken, Smitten, Afflicted, Wounded,
Carries, Sorrows, Chastised, Laid, Offered, Pierced, Oppressed,

Slaughter, Cut, Bruised, Poured, Death, Grieved, Offered, Labored, Served, Numbered, Bore, Intercession, Justified, Satisfied.

Each of those are mostly verbs and are what your Savior has done for you. That is how much He loves you. Thanks be to God.

Isaiah 53:

Who has believed our report?
And to whom has the arm of the LORD been revealed?
For He shall grow up before Him as a tender plant,
And as a root out of dry ground.

He has no form or comeliness;
And when we see Him,
There is no beauty that we should desire Him.
He is despised and rejected by men,
A Man of sorrows and acquainted with grief.
And we hid, as it were, *our* faces from Him;
He was despised, and we did not esteem Him.

Surely He has borne our griefs
And carried our sorrows;
Yet we esteemed Him stricken,
Smitten by God, and afflicted.
But He *was* wounded for our transgressions,
He was bruised for our iniquities;
The chastisement for our peace *was* upon Him,
And by His stripes we are healed.
All we like sheep have gone astray;
We have turned, every one, to his own way;
And the LORD has laid on Him the iniquity of us all.

He was oppressed and He was afflicted,
Yet He opened not His mouth;
He was led as a lamb to the slaughter,
And as a sheep before its shearers is silent,
So He opened not His mouth.
He was taken from prison and from judgment,
And who will declare His generation?
For He was cut off from the land of the living;
For the transgressions of My people He was stricken.
And they made His grave with the wicked—
But with the rich at His death,
Because He had done no violence,
Nor *was any* deceit in His mouth.

Yet it pleased the Lord to bruise Him;
He has put *Him* to grief.
When You make His soul an offering for sin,
He shall see *His* seed, He shall prolong *His* days,
And the pleasure of the Lord shall prosper in His hand.
He shall see the labor of His soul, *and* be satisfied.
By His knowledge My righteous Servant shall justify many,
For He shall bear their iniquities.
Therefore I will divide Him a portion with the great,
And He shall divide the spoil with the strong,
Because He poured out His soul unto death,
And He was numbered with the transgressors,
And He bore the sin of many,
And made intercession for the transgressors.

Isaiah 53:5 (Old Testament) But He was wounded for our transgressions. He was bruised for our iniquities; The chastisement for our peace was upon Him. And by His stripes we are healed.

Isaiah 53:7 (Old Testament) He was led as a lamb to the slaughter, and as a sheep before it's shearers is silent.

CHAPTER 10

Correlation and Context

Correlation and context are very important to discovering the undeniable relevance of the bible. They are two characteristics that always stand out when studying the bible and its correlation and context. The word correlation was originated in the 16th century from Medieval Latin.

Correlation is basically described as a neutral relationship of connection between two or more things.

The following definition is provided by Wikipedia.com:

*In the broadest sense **correlation** is any statistical association, though in common usage it most often refers to how close two variables are to having a <u>linear relationship</u> with each other.*

There are basically three types of correlation. They are positive, negative, and no correlation. Often times you may have a direct correlation or an indirect correlation. For instance, there is a correlation between cigarette smoking and lung cancer. Unfortunately, this is a direct correlation.

The next characteristic we will examine is context. Context is defined as the circumstances that form the setting for an event, statement or idea and in terms of which it can be fully understood and assessed. In terms of writing, it becomes the why and how a situation presents itself. So, context is situational in its relationship.

Below is the listed definition of context from oxforddictionaries.com

The parts of something written or spoken that immediately precede and follow a word or passage and clarify its meaning.

'skilled readers use context to construct meaning from words as they are read'

> **Ephesians 6:17 and the helmet of salvation, and the sword of the Spirit, which is the word of God.**

CHAPTER 11

God's Love Note

Perhaps you have either given or received a love note in your lifetime. Perhaps it was when you were in school. Hopefully, it was offered to someone who struck your fancy. Maybe even you struck theirs.

The level of the Bible's authenticity reaches unmatched proportion. There really is nothing comparable to the love that God has for each and every one of us.

It has been said that love makes the world go around. What an understatement! Where would any of us be without love? Probably really lost. So, without it I think we would be in trouble. The love that we share with each other is so very powerful, joyful and more than that the love we have for the Lord makes all the difference in our lives. God does indeed love us so very much. Love is indeed everything. Knowing just how much God loves us and then in turn loving Him back certainly makes all the difference. It truly does, and it manifests itself in how we treat each other and ultimately love one another. You come to the realization that the same God that made you made another. The very same God which makes all of us brothers and sisters. We are not so very different, we just think that we are. God is so very good that often it is difficult to contemplate the magnitude of His love for us which is completely and absolutely enormous. Perhaps difficult for many to even understand. God's love is downright enormous and completely outstanding.

The Greek term agape love is often used when describing the kind of love that God has for us. It is an unconditional love that truly has no bounds. It is the kind of love that all of us should strive for, but only God is capable of, because He does not have the human limitations that we are subject to. Our human selfish nature only gets in the way. We are actually in the way. We need to understand that ultimately, we cannot and do not love in the same capacity that He loves. We try, and we ultimately fail. We are given the greatest example of all in that Jesus loved us so very much that He went to the cross to pay for our sins. So, indeed if we are to manifest that Christian love, then we need to love thoroughly with all of our hearts and put our selfish needs aside and think of others before we think of ourselves. Can you put the needs of another in front of your own? Very difficult to do most of the time, but completely necessary. Even to forgive each other and even to forgive what we might define or label as unforgivable. There is no such thing if God is willing to forgive you of all your sins and He says He will not even remember them. In turn we need to forgive our brother and moreover we need to love them completely and wholeheartedly with absolutely no hesitation or limitation. When you truly love someone, it becomes the greatest feeling in the world. Live by example and most importantly, love by example. How will they know we are Christians? They will know by our love. It truly does not get any better than that.

There are four types of love found in the Bible. They are represented by four Greek words. They are Eros, Storge, Philia, and Agape. Eros is defined as a romantic love. A love that exists between a couple. Storge is defined as a family love, in this case it would be the love for parents or the love for your children. Philia is defined as brotherly love. This also is displayed as Christian love. Finally, we have agape which is God's divine, unconditional love.

> **Romans 8:37 Yet in all these things we are more than conquerors through Him who loved us.**

CHAPTER 12

The Godhead

The Godhead. Do you know it, and do you understand it? More importantly, do you believe in it and do you live it? That is certainly the very most important part. I think most people have an image of an older man as the image of our Father in Heaven. I know that often I picture this older father figure in my mind. However, God is not one person but actually three people existing within God. We have a plural God. Probably difficult to completely comprehend from our human perspective. Everything with God happens for a reason. For His reason and while many times it does not seem so, all things work for good. He had to come here as a man (Jesus) and save all of mankind. So, God is the Father and He is the Son and He is the Holy Spirit. Jesus tells the apostles I am leaving behind a Helper (the Holy Spirit) for you. God calls Himself I AM and what comes after the I AM .... Well basically everything. I AM everything. He certainly IS everything. All that matters anyway. Jesus was there from the very beginning, but He came to earth 2018 years ago and it is where we get AD (Anno Domini) meaning in the year of His birth. Try to comprehend that with God anything can and does happen. He is not limited by any human limitation as we are limited in so many ways. Remember in the Gospels when Jesus raises His hand and calms the seas and the wind. The Apostles look at each other and say who can this be that even the sea and wind obey? He is indeed the great I AM. In Hebrews 1 verse 8, God calls Jesus God and references His scepter of righteousness. So here again God exists in three distinct persons. When Jesus is baptized by John the Baptist all three beings of God are present as the dove (the Holy Spirit) descends on Jesus, the Son, and the clouds open and God the Father's voice calls out that this is my beloved Son in whom I am well pleased. We have a plural God. Moreover, we have an amazing and incredibly loving God. A God who takes away our sin and transgressions by the power of the cross.

God exists in three persons: The Father, The Son and the Holy Spirit. Jesus is the right hand man of God. He does the Father's will. He is the savior that everyone needs and that everyone has. He sits at the right of God the Father for all eternity and is part of the incredible Godhead.

Often times we depend on someone that we can trust and count on completely, and we refer to that person as our right hand man. We know we can depend on that person to do what is in our best interest at all times. That someone has our back in every situation. That person is someone you would trust with your life and beyond any measure. In some ways they actually become part of our purpose and commitment. They can assist us in the manifestation of our responsibility, utility and usefulness. We know ahead of time that we can trust this person in every sense. Ultimately, Jesus becomes the right hand man for each and every one of us. He is God's right hand man and He is our right hand man. Could there ever be a bigger blessing than that? We are able to lean on Him knowing all the time that He is there for us and will never turn away from us. He loves us so very much. He has our back at all times. He holds us up when we are in times of turmoil, tragedy, despair, disease and hopelessness. With Him in our corner and as our right hand we can be assured that we will always have hope. It is a love, commitment and a hope that no one else can ever give us. We rely on Him to take our sin from us and to provide eternal life for us. He is always there for us and never lets us down, even when we let ourselves down. He is our right hand man in every way imaginable.

So, if He is always there for us, shouldn't we always be there for Him. He loves us so much and we need to show Him that we also love Him. He is after all our great right hand man. He wants us to love each other and be kind to one another. He tells the apostles that they showed Him love, and they ask Him when did we do those things? He answers, when you have done it to the least of you then you have done it for Me. Once again, His agape love is on display in every way each and every day.

Jesus is the second part of the Godhead. God is manifested as a human through the person of Jesus Christ. What an incredible Lord that we have.

Micah 5:7 But you Bethlehem Ephrathah, though you were little among the thousands of Judah, Yet out of you shall come forth to Me the one to be ruler in Israel, Whose going forths are from old, from everlasting.

CHAPTER 13

History and Archaeology

We are nothing but mere humans which means we are mere sinners. We are born into this humanness. We cannot help our sinful nature. We cannot help our sinful selves. We are sinners through and through. We are servants. We are His servants and we are blessed to be those servants. I have been and always will be a history guy. I love history and always have. It is so very important to know where indeed we came from. It is completely compelling and at times can be even somewhat overwhelming. Although it is overwhelming in a good way. History comes down to fact. It is not opinion. It is truth. The God honest truth. These people and events actually took place. So, history and archaeology are so very compelling. Two items in archaeology that always stand out to me are the Tel Dan Inscription and the Pilate Stone. There are many, many others and of course the great prophesy of the Bible itself. History is something that has already occurred. It has already happened. It cannot be erased. It cannot be changed. It cannot be argued. It cannot be altered. These things occurred. They happened. These findings are unarguable examples that these people were real and that they were here. Right here. So, what does one do with this history? What does one do with this truth? Does one really need a stone tablet to fall on our heads? (Pun intended). Sometimes I think the world does not get it because the world does not want to get it. Sort of like the Pharisees. They did not want to get it. Jesus was bad for business. He truly was. Maybe they actually did know who He was but did not want to conform to God Himself. Human nature is just that; it is human before it is anything else. Knowing God requires humility and it requires us making ourselves secondary. They were not going to be bypassed because of a "Carpenter from Nazareth". Their pride actually got in the way of their faith. There is nothing holy about being human. Absolutely nothing. God alone is holy, and we certainly are not. Let us examine some of this great history and archaeology that the world wants to ignore. It is vital to our very being and our very existence. It is vital to our eternal souls. The truth shall set you free.

The Tel Dan Inscription

The Tel Dan inscription is an archaeological find that illustrates the existence of King David, the House of David and the Line of David. There was such an Israeli King. This finding is of utmost importance when one is researching the historicity and lineage of both King David and that of Jesus Himself.

Taken from Biblehistorydaily.com:

Few modern Biblical archaeology discoveries have caused as much excitement as the Tel Dan inscription—writing on a ninth-century B.C. stone slab (or stela) that furnished the first historical evidence of King David from the Bible.

The Tel Dan inscription, or "House of David" inscription, was discovered in 1993 at the site of Tel Dan in northern Israel in an excavation directed by Israeli archaeologist Avraham Biran.

The broken and fragmentary inscription commemorates the victory of an Aramean king over his two southern neighbors: the "king of Israel" and the "king of the House of David." In the carefully incised text written in neat Aramaic characters, the Aramean king boasts that he, under the divine guidance of the god Hadad, vanquished several thousand Israelite and Judahite horsemen and charioteers before personally dispatching both of his royal opponents. Unfortunately, the recovered fragments of the "House of David" inscription do not preserve the names of the specific kings involved in this brutal encounter, but most scholars believe the stela recounts a campaign of Hazael of Damascus in which he defeated both Jehoram of Israel and Ahaziah of Judah.

What made the Tel Dan inscription one of the most exciting Biblical archaeology discoveries for scholars and the broader public was its unprecedented reference to the "House of David." The stela's fragmented inscription, first read and translated by the renowned epigrapher Joseph Naveh, proved that King David from the Bible was a genuine historical figure and not simply the fantastic literary creation of later Biblical writers and editors. Perhaps more important, the stela, set up by one of ancient Israel's fiercest enemies more than a century after David's death, still recognized David as the founder of the kingdom of Judah.

The Pilate Stone

The Pilate stone, found in 1961, shows the existence of the Roman Governor, Pontius Pilate and the stone he dedicated to the then emperor, Tiberius. Once again found archaeology that science both cannot deny and cannot dispute. In fact, science does not even attempt to explain these findings. It does not attempt because it simply cannot. Pilate was an actual Roman procurator who served in Judea from 26 AD to 36 AD. You cannot get around the truth. Truth is truth.

After considering this great archaeology and history, and

hearing so many call our faith blind faith, I am not sure there is anything blind about it. Not a single thing. Truth is truth and facts are facts. It is the obvious truth. History and archaeology illustrate where we have been, where we are currently, and where we are going. They are not opinions, but they are indeed facts. Just curious but what does a non-believer do with this archaeology, history and Bible prophesy? These events took place. It is all truth. The truth is evident. The truth shall set us free.

The following text is from www.bible-history.com:

The Bible clearly mentions Pontius Pilate as the Roman procurator of Judea at the time of Jesus Christ. Since this dedication stone found in Caesarea Maritima was the first inscription mentioning his actual name, and that he indeed was the Roman procurator who had made his official residence in Caesarea, the discovery of The Pilate Inscription is a monumental discovery that verifies again that the Bible is a Book of history.

> *James 1:18* **Of his own will he brought us forth by the word of truth, that we should be a kind of first fruits of his creatures.**

CHAPTER 14

Cornerstone

Cornerstone is a word which defines and denotes foundation and base. We need structure and stability in our daily lives. We need it badly and often depend on structure and balance. God provides that structure and stability through our Lord and savior, Jesus Christ. He is the ultimate cornerstone. Who, and, or what is the cornerstone foundation of your life? Cornerstone is defined as a stone that forms the base of a corner of a building joining two walls together. Another definition is as an important quality or feature on which a particular thing depends or is based.

Also, the foundation stone concept is based on the first set stone in the construction phase of a masonry foundation. It is vital since all of the other accompanying stones will be set in relation and reference to this stone, in essence determining the position of the entire structure.

So, then what is it that becomes your bedrock or your cornerstone? In other words where do you derive your stability? This must in fact depend on your faith. For in your faith you will find all that you need for your earthly as well as eternal survival. Do not lean on you, but rather lean on Him. He will hold you up and He will raise you up in times of tribulation and storm. God tells us that His grace is sufficient. Once you confidently believe that Jesus is there for you now and forever, then he becomes your ultimate cornerstone. That is the love of our God. It is rock solid. He is our cornerstone and our salvation. He tells us to abide in Him and He will abide in us. Jesus loves you and that is certain. Love Him with everything that you are, and it will make the biggest difference in your life. Indeed, the only way to the Father is through the Son. Get close to God and you will get your cornerstone. He is all that we ever need.

> *Ephesians 2:20 Having been built on the foundation of the apostles and prophets, Jesus Christ Himself being the chief cornerstone.*

CHAPTER 15

My Words Will
Never Fade Away

Sometimes my thoughts can wonder to those of us who CHOOSE not to believe. I wonder to myself how can that even be? My heart actually hurts for these people. When God says they will be without excuse, He really means it. Jesus tells us that my words will never pass away, and I guess that is why we still have and always will have the Bible. Yet, people will always try to find fault with it, and they will try to doubt its authorship and its authentication. Here is the thing though. You cannot change prophesy and history that has been around for many thousands of years, and also you cannot change all of the things that Jesus says will happen. They end up happening exactly just as He says they will happen. The temple for instance. Coincidence? I think not! Israel becoming a nation again on May 14, 1948. Moreover, stop and realize the reality of our own mortality. Simply stated, we all someday will stop breathing and will die. Nothing will be left of us but a fleeting memory. Our legacy will not endure, and we will indeed be like the wind. Yet, His legacy outlasts time. Consider that. You will fade away, but He will never fade away. No, not ever. Jesus indeed lives and He alone indeed saves. You will be long gone, and they will still be talking about Jesus. He is our Savior yesterday, today, tomorrow and forever. I guess it really comes down to hope. From a practical standpoint without Jesus interceding for our sin, we are stuck in it. It would stick to us like glue, and there would be no answer for sin. Ultimately, we would die in our sin, and never have any hope of Heaven. There would be no hope of salvation whatsoever. God had to come as a man and be sacrificed for our sin. In Jesus we have the perfect Lamb who is without blemish. He takes our sin away. God not only forgives our sin, but He also forgets it. I for one want to spend eternity with Him and be in that number. I want to accept this special gift that only He could provide.

So, I am left with praying for those nonbelievers and praying for the fence sitters. You cannot have it both ways. I had heard it said before that if you believe then this world is as bad as it will ever get. Contrarily, if you do not believe, then this world is as good as it will ever get. God says you are either for me or against me. There is no middle. He says he has no room for lukewarm people. Try to do things His way rather than your way. He knows everything and even knows you better than you know you.

Matthew 24:35 Heaven and Earth will pass away, but My words will by no means pass away.

CHAPTER 16

A Poor Jewish Carpenter

Try to consider and contemplate that the most famous person in all of history is a poor Jewish carpenter. That is right. Jesus Christ is the most famous person in all of history. Who else's life changed both history and time. It is a certainty. It is undeniable. There is no way around it and there is no doubt about it. God gives us all of the answers to all of the questions throughout the Bible. We just have to become better evaluators and better listeners. Why are we so dense? Our entire system of time is based on the life of Jesus. What year are you in? 2,018 represents 2,018 years after the birth of Jesus Christ. AD does not mean after death like some people believe but rather it means Anno Domini which is Latin for in the year of our Lord. So, our entire time system is based on His birth and His life. Religious or not, you have to try to grasp the fact that God came as a man and in doing so, He changed the world and time as we know it forevermore. He loves us so much that even in our doubt and weakness of faith, He alone provides all the answers. He is the answer for yesterday, today and tomorrow. We have such an incredible God. Whether we are able to see it and comprehend it really is entirely up to us. I am a believer and that is easy to see but I would argue that based on all the factual information, archaeology, history and Bible prophesy that it is much more difficult to be a non-believer. History is a compilation of events that have already happened, and these events show us where we have come from, where we are currently and more importantly where we are going. This life is the temporal one. It is completely temporary. So, examine the history and try to explain how a poor Jewish carpenter can change time forever and how He is manifested in our everyday lives whether we can see it or not. My prayer would be that each and every person would see it and recognize it for exactly what it is. In this case pure grace. Everything Jesus says will happen, happens just as He says it will be including His death and His resurrection. He tells us that His words will never pass away, and they never do. God does everything for a reason; His reason. Read the Bible, understand it and try to do the most challenging thing for all of us, live it! Below are some verses I think are most telling and are indeed prophesies. There are so many more. Try and get to know the Savior, the most famous person in all of history and all of humanity. He always was (In the beginning was the Word), He always is (I am), and He always will be (Revelation He is coming again). Are you able to contemplate just how much He loves you? Contemplate that long after you and I are just a distant memory that they will still be talking about Jesus and what He did for mankind and what He does every single day. He loves you. There is nothing like it. God is indeed so very good. He is great!

> **Isaiah 43:25 I, even, I, am He who blots out your transgressions for my own sake; And I will not remember your sins.**

CHAPTER 17

Good from Nazareth?

Philip states, "We have found Him of Moses, in the law, and also the prophets wrote – Jesus of Nazareth, the son of Joseph." Nathaniel asks Philip: Can anything good come from Nazareth? Philip says, "Come and See."

Jesus was actually born in Bethlehem (the city of David) however, he grew up in Nazareth. Nazareth was considered working class. It consisted of average people with average intellect. For the most part, its citizens were uneducated people and often tradesman. Jesus was a carpenter. Nazareth is located in the province of Galilee. Israel has three provinces in total. The other two are named Samaria and Judea.

Galilee is the northern most province in Israel. Sometimes, Jesus is referred to as "the Galilean". Thus, the Messiah is often referred to as the Nazarene or the Galilean.

The following definition is from Wikipedia:

The Nazarenes originated as a sect of first-century Judaism. The first use of the term "sect of the Nazarenes" is in the Book of Acts in the New Testament, where Paul is accused of being a ringleader of the sect of the Nazarenes ("πρωτοστάτην τε τῆς τῶν Ναζωραίων αἱρέσεως").

Then, the term simply designated followers of "Yeshua Natzri" (Jesus the Nazarene), as the Hebrew term יְרֹצוֹנ (nôṣrî) still does, but in the first to fourth centuries, the term was used for a sect of followers of Jesus who were closer to Judaism than most Christians. They are described by Epiphanius of Salamis and are mentioned later by Jerome and Augustine of Hippo. The writers made a distinction between the Nazarenes of their time and the "Nazarenes" mentioned in Acts 24:5, where Paul the Apostle is accused before Felix at Caesarea (the capital of Roman Judaea) by Tertullus.

These are some words from the song "Put your hand in the hand of the Man from Galilee":

Put your hand in the hand of the man who stilled the waters
Put your hand in the hand of the man who calmed the sea
Take a look at yourself and you can look at the others differently
By puttin' your hand in the hand of the man from Galilee

Mama taught me how to pray before I reached the age of seven
And when I'm down on my knees that's when I'm closest to heaven
Daddy lived his life for eight kids and a wife you do what you must do
But he showed me enough of what it takes to get you through

So, something very good did come from Nazareth. The Messiah Himself.

Matthew 2:22 But when he (Joseph) heard that Archelaus was reigning in Judea in place of his father Herod, he was afraid to go there. Having been warned in a dream, he (Joseph) withdrew

to the district of Galilee, and he went and lived in a town called Nazareth. So was fulfilled what was said through the prophets: "He (Jesus) will be called a Nazarene."

CHAPTER 18

The Good Shepherd

The word shepherd means someone who guards and keeps the sheep. Jesus is the ultimate good shepherd to each and every one of us.

The word shepherd derives from old English. In John 21:17 Jesus is speaking to Peter (mind you post resurrection) and tells Peter to feed my sheep.

So, Jesus is the ultimate shepherd and we are ultimately His sheep. Jesus also states "I am the good shepherd. The good shepherd gives His life for the sheep."

He said to him the third time, "Simon, *son* of Jonah, do you love me?" Peter was grieved because He said to him the third time, "Do you love Me?"

And he said to Him, "Lord, You know all things; You know that I love You."

Jesus said to him, "Feed My sheep."

"I am the good shepherd. The good shepherd gives His life for the sheep."

"Therefore, My Father loves Me, because I lay down My life that I may take it again. No one takes it from Me, but I lay it down of Myself. I have power to lay it down, and I have power to take it again. This command I have received from My Father."

No Greater love has no one than this, than to lay down one's life for his friends. You are My friends if you do whatever I command you. No longer do I call you servants, for a servant does not know what his master is doing; but I have called you friends, for all things that I heard from My Father I have made known to you. You did not choose Me, but I chose you and appointed you that you should go and bear fruit, and *that* your fruit should remain, that whatever you ask the Father in My name He may give you.

John 10:11 "I am the good shepherd. The good shepherd gives His life for the sheep.

Chapter 19

Hope

Maybe you think there are times when all is lost. It never is though. When you have Jesus, you have hope. Without Jesus there is no hope. Merely look at the state of the world and you can clearly see that. The difference in a person's life seems to clearly be attributed and associated to their faith. We all have so very much work to do and yet with the hope that Jesus alone has provided, we can be bound for Heaven. We certainly do not deserve Heaven. Every single one of us is a wretch. We are born into it. Truth be told we deserve the other place, but with Jesus there is always hope. He provides it, and only He provides it. If you ever see a Christian or any person for that matter who thinks they are in a good place, then they need to start all over. None are good, no, not even one. So, the hope lies in Him and Him alone.

Our hope rests in Christ and in Christ alone. As He says, "With God anything is possible." He is there for us and He is always there for us. When you have Christ in your life, you will always have hope.

Consider and reflect on this definition of hope: **hope** is an optimistic attitude of mind that is based on an expectation of positive outcomes related to events and circumstances in one's life or the world at large. As a verb, its definitions include: "expect with confidence" and "to cherish a desire with anticipation".

That is a Jesus thing and there is no doubt about it. It is why He left behind His incredible teachings and His incredible example of Love.

The following definition is from Merriam Webster dictionary

Definition of HOPE

hoped; **hoping**

<u>intransitive verb</u>
1: to cherish a desire with anticipation: to want something to happen or be true
- *hopes* for a promotion
- *hoping* for the best
- I *hope* so.

2*archaic*: <u>TRUST</u>

<u>transitive verb</u>

1: to desire with expectation of obtainment or fulfillment
- I *hope* she remembers.
- *hopes* to be invited

2: to expect with confidence: <u>TRUST</u>
- Your mother is doing well, I *hope*.

> **1 Peter 1:3 Blessed *be* the God and Father of our Lord Jesus Christ, who according to His abundant mercy has begotten us again to a living hope through the resurrection of Jesus**

Christ from the dead, [4] to an inheritance incorruptible and undefiled and that does not fade away, reserved in heaven for you, [5] who are kept by the power of God through faith for salvation ready to be revealed in the last time.

CHAPTER 20

The Greatest Teacher

Jesus Christ is the greatest teacher of all time. He teaches us by His ways, by His words, and by His incredible example. Perhaps instead of "what would Jesus do?" it should be "what would Jesus have me do?"

The following definition is provided by merriamwebster.com:

Definition of TEACH
taught play \ˈtȯt\; teaching
transitive verb

1a: to cause to know something
• *taught* them a trade
b: to cause to know how
• is *teaching* me to drive
c: to accustom to some action or attitude
• *teach* students to think for themselves
d: to cause to know the disagreeable consequences of some action
• I'll *teach* you to come home late
2: to guide the studies of
3: to impart the knowledge of

- *teach* algebra

4a: to instruct by precept, example, or experience

b: to make known and accepted

- experience *teaches* us our limitations

5: to conduct instruction regularly in

- *teach* school

Many times throughout the Bible Jesus is often referred to as teacher or master. The apostles were more than willing to serve a subservient role when it came to Jesus the Christ. Jesus illustrates His love and commitment to all peoples for all time. Jesus would not have been considered an educated person or scholarly for the time. He was by profession a simple carpenter. Yet, he knows scriptures. Many times, he asks, "have you not read?" The scribes and Pharisees could not contemplate how it was that Jesus knew so very much. Often times they tried to test him. They were unsuccessful in their attempts.

The following excerpt is taken from the book Rediscover Jesus, by Matthew Kelly, pgs. 50 & 51.

Spiritual leaders of all types throughout history have often complicated the path to God in ways that have made it almost impossible for the average person to walk the path. God gave Moses the Ten Commandments. By the time of Jesus, these had evolved into 613 laws. The simplicity of Jesus' teaching was radical in contrast to the stifling effect these 613 laws had on daily life.

The content of his teachings was radical because it focused on conversion of the heart rather than external behaviors. The method of his teachings was radical because his primary teaching tool was the parable. He used stories and metaphors that ordinary people could understand. This meant that his teachings were accessible and practical to ordinary people, especially the uneducated.

Also, from the book Rediscover Jesus by Matthew Kelly, pg. 62.

Forgiveness and generosity are two of the most radical challenges Jesus levels at us. They are at once incredibly spiritual and monumentally practical. Our willingness to give and forgive often reveals the depth, or limitations, of our Christianity.

> **Exodus 14: 14 "So it should be, when your son asks you in time to come, saying, "what is this? That you should say to him, "By strength of hand the Lord brought us out of Egypt, out of the house of bondage."**

CHAPTER 21

Salvation and Sanctification

Salvation and sanctification are indeed two of the most important factors to our faith.

The following text comes from activechristianity.org

Justification, salvation and sanctification

Justification – forgiveness, the clearing of all of my guilt and the deserved penalty for committed sins, through faith in Jesus Christ, who took on the penalty for my sins and paid the price by dying in my stead. (Galatians 2:16) This leads to salvation.

Salvation – saved from the penalty of committed sin, but – even greater – also from the very root of sin; from the bondage I was in to the body of sin. (Hebrews 7:19, 25) The Holy Spirit comes to dwell in me and works in me, leading me to overcome sin is anything that goes against God's will and His laws. To commit sin is to transgress or disobey these laws. The lust to sin dwells in human nature. In other words, it is contaminated and motivated by the sinful tendencies that dwell in all people as a result of the fall into sin and disobedience in the garden of

Eden. This... More before it is committed. I am saved from the necessity
of committing sin just because I have sin – which leads to ...

Sanctification – This is the result of salvation. It is the transformation.
This is the process of sanctification, in which we our sinful human
nature is gradually exchanged for divine nature when we in obedience to
God's will deny and put to death the sinful lusts in our flesh. (Romans
12:2; 2 Corinthians 3:18; 2 Peter 1:3-4)... More from human to divine
nature, God's nature, or divine nature, is perfectly pure and it cannot
be tempted by evil. We are promised that we can be partakers of the
divine nature by fleeing the corruption in the world that comes through
our lusts. As we gradually overcome our sinful human nature it is
replaced by divine nature – God shares His own nature with... More (2
Peter 1:2-4; 1 Peter 1:15-16; Matthew 5:48); being made holy. This is a
process I undergo throughout my lifetime as I, in obedience to the Spirit,
put off the flesh Conscious sin; things we know to be sin before we do
them. These are not "accidents" but deliberate sins, and they are to be
repented from and "put off" at conversion: "Now the works of the flesh
are evident, which are: adultery, fornication, uncleanness, lewdness,
idolatry, sorcery, hatred, contentions, jealousies, outbursts of wrath,
selfish ambitions, dissensions, heresies, envy, murders, drunkenness,...
More and take on the fruit of the Spirit. (Galatians 5:16-16)

Of course, this is all by grace. By grace God worked in my heart, calling
me to repentance is the act of regretting sincerely the sin in your past
with the goal to never do it again. It is making a decision to turn away
from evil and to serve God. Repentance is one of the requirements for
the forgiveness of sins. (Mark 2:17; Luke 15:10; Luke 24:46-47; Acts 3:19;
Romans 2:4; 2 Corinthians 7:10; 2 Peter... More. By grace and obedience
to the faith, as a disciple. A disciple is another word for a follower of
Christ, one who is learning to be like his Master. As a disciple you
follow Jesus Christ, who is the Master and by living like Him you
become more like Him. (Matthew 16:24; 1 Peter 2:21-22)... More, I am

saved, sanctified, made holy, and purified as He, my Master, Savior, and Bridegroom, is pure.

The following excerpt is taken from Rediscover Jesus by Matthew Kelly pg. 171:

A holy moment is a moment when you are being the person God created you to be, and you are doing what you feel God is calling you to do in that moment.

The following commentary is from en.m.wikibooks.org

Looking at salvation by grace through faith which is not of our works but God who did it for us as a human race. Ephesians 2:8 and 9 adds on and says that none should boast because we do not save our self except for the grace of God. Our part is to use faith to take what is ours (salvation), we do not deserve to perish, the fire in hell is been made for the devil and his angels from the beginning of all wars that are heavenly. Then shall he say also unto them on the left hand, depart from me, ye cursed, into everlasting fire, prepared for the devil and his angels: Mathew 25 vs 41. Faith is our part to play believing in what you have never seen but you are convicted of its existence. The world was created by faith by Him from whom all things began.

We are not holy. You are not holy. I am not holy. Only Jesus is holy. His holiness is what provides both our salvation and sanctification. There is nothing that any human can do to earn heaven. It has been earned for us, and it is accessible only through the sacrifice of Jesus Christ.

Acts 26:18 To open their eyes, and to turn them from darkness to light, and from the power of Satan unto God, that they may receive

forgiveness of sins, and inheritance among them which are sanctified by faith that is in me.

CHAPTER 22

I And the Father Are One

We have a triune God; the Father, the Son and the Holy Spirit. Three in one and one in all three. We have a plural God. This sometimes is difficult for some to grasp and understand, but you must say to yourself that God can do and does do anything. He can be anywhere and everywhere at any time and at the same time. Omnipresent without our human limitations. Genesis 1:26. Then God said, "Let US make man in Our image, according to Our likeness. ..." This implies a plural God, not a singular one. Again, three in one and one in three. Present at creation, were God the Father, God the Son, and God the Holy Spirit. Jesus was there from the beginning. Also, from John, In the beginning was the Word and the Word was with God and the Word was God. From John 10:30, I and the Father are one. Colossians 2:9 For in Him (Jesus) dwelleth all the fullness of the Godhead bodily. 1st John 5:7 "For there are three that bear record in Heaven, the Father, the Word, and the Holy Ghost: and THESE THREE ARE ONE." Here is one where God the Father calls Jesus God. Hebrews 1:8 But unto the Son God saith, "Thy throne, O God, is forever and ever: a scepter of righteousness is the scepter of thy kingdom." 1st John 4:10 "Herein is love, not that we loved God, but that He loved us, and sent His son to be the propitiation for our sins." There are so many other references existing in the Old Testament (pre-incarnate,) and the New Testament (Jesus among us). Ultimately though without a savior to take on our sin, none of us will ever make it. We simply cannot do it ourselves and we would remain in our sin. All of us would be stuck in our sin. We are not holy He is. We needed the perfect Lamb to take our sin away from us and that is what God supplies. Our God is magnificent and so very loving. The Godhead is the Father, the Son and the Spirit.

This indeed is crucial to our salvation to understand that only the blood of the perfect lamb (Jesus) can save us from ourselves. He IS God ... The great I AM, the King of kings and The Lord of lords. He tells the apostles, "When you have seen Me you have seen the Father." No one comes to the Father except through the Son. Not a single person. No amount of good works or any other earthly thing will ever save you. Jesus and only Jesus saves. You would die in your sins and could not possibly gain Heaven. Jesus alone saves us. He is the way, the truth and the life. He alone is our hope. He alone is our salvation. He is the hope of the world. Get to know Him and do things His way instead of your way. God saves, so let Him save you. It will make all of the difference in the world when you give him the reins so to speak to guide your life.

The only way to the Father is through the Son. The one and only way. What an amazing, incredible and loving God that we have........ Wow! He is amazing. What a wonderful blessing!

Genesis 1: 26 Then God said, "Let us make man in Our image, according to Our likeness; let them have dominion over the fish of the sea, over the birds of the air, and over the cattle, over all the earth and over every creeping thing that creeps on the earth."

CHAPTER 23

God Is Love

Nothing can compare to God's love. There is simply nothing in existence that is even close. It has been said many times that the closest we would ever know to God's love is that of a mother's love to their child.

The Bible demonstrates explicitly the complete enormity of God's love.

So, it all comes down to self-sacrifice. Love is being able to put other's needs in front of your own. When you are in love everything around you seems nicer, softer, smells better, tastes better, etc, etc.

It is not about you. It is about Him, what He did and His incredible gift to each and every one of us. We do not deserve grace but that is exactly what He gave us. He wants us not to be selfish, but to be selfless. It is for us to be actually more like Him. That is what He intends. It is a prayer on how we should treat each other and how God wants us to be unselfish, loving and self-sacrificing. Jesus is indeed the ultimate model of sacrifice. His example is unmatched. The Bible says those who are first will be last, and those who are last will be first. Prayer is so powerful and can be so very inspirational. This indeed illustrates that God wants us to be humble and to honor Him and each other in that humility. We need to be humble consistently and constantly. We need to strive to do things God's way rather than our way. To help others rather than being so very self-consumed. In doing so we can become closer to God. This prayer is from St Francis of Assisi:

Lord,
Make me an instrument of your peace;
Where there is hatred, let me sow love;
Where there is injury, pardon;
Where there is doubt, faith;
Where there is despair, hope;
Where there is darkness, light;
Where there is sadness, joy.
O Divine Master,
Grant that I may not so much seek to be consoled as to console;
To be understood as to understand; To be loved as to love.
For it is in giving that we receive.
It is in pardoning that we are pardoned
It is in dying that we are born to eternal life.

The following comment is from biblestudytools.com:

God is love and has demonstrated that love in everything that he does. Paul compares faith, hope, and love, and concludes that "the greatest of these is love" (1 Cor 13:13).

"God Is Love. "Agape [ajgavph], the love theme of the Bible, can only be defined by the nature of God. John affirms that "God is love" (1 John 4:8). God does not merely love; he is love. Everything that God does flows from his love.

It has been said that love makes the world go around. It truly does in every sense. God's love is amazing love. In the Latin the term is "agape" meaning never ending love. It becomes an epiphany when you realize the lengths that God goes to save us. That is exactly what it is. It is never ending. Sometimes it is so amazing to come to the realization and magnitude of God's love for us. There have been many times in my life where it is so overwhelming that I get chills. They are good chills but still chills nonetheless. Left to our own accord, none of us will make it. No, not even one. We would all be in very big trouble. We are all sinners and could not even begin to comprehend holiness or divinity in any way, shape or form. There is nothing holy about being human. Absolutely nothing. We are stuck in a very human and very sinful condition. All we ever do is want more and we complain if we do not get our way. We are really pretty pathetic when you think about it. Completely and utterly spoiled. All throughout the Bible there is offering for sin all the way back to the first Passover in Exodus. They took the blood of a PERFECT LAMB and placed the blood on the top, sides and bottom of the doorway (that forms a cross). Frankly, we do not deserve Heaven. You cannot earn Heaven as it has been earned for you. It is grace and is downright incredible. What an awesome gift. We are not worthy, yet God loves us so very much that He gives us Jesus. He goes to the cross for us. He gives His life for us. Jesus' last words on the cross were Tetelestai, meaning "It is finished." He has done it so that we can have Heaven. It comes down to God wanted His family back. That is how much He loves us. So much so that He gave His own life. It is a love that is unconditional, unconscionable, unmatched, undeniable and for us completely undeserved. A love that can only be achieved by the Almighty One, our Creator, the Lord above. He is so incredible. Why He would do what He does for all of us I cannot even begin to fathom or explain, but I sure am glad that He did. He loves us so immensely. It is the most wonderful blessing He has bestowed on ALL of us.

> **Romans 8:39 Nor height, nor depth, nor any other creature, shall be able to separate us from the love of God, which is in Christ Jesus, our Lord.**

> **Isaiah 53:6 All we like sheep have gone astray; We have turned, everyone, to his own way; And the Lord has laid on Him the iniquity of us all.**

CHAPTER 24

The Wind and The Sea Obey?

Here comes another understatement: Jesus is great, and He can do anything.

The setting is this, all twelve apostles and Jesus are in the sea of Galilee in a boat. A great windstorm arises. The waves are beating into the boat as it was filling up with water. But he was asleep in the stern on a pillow. The apostles awake him and say to him "teacher, do you not care that we are perishing?" Then he arose and rebuked the wind, and said to the sea "Peace, be still!" And the wind ceased and there was a great calm. But he said to them, "Why are you so fearful?" "How is it that you have no faith?" And they feared exceedingly, and said to one another "Who can this be, that even the wind and the sea obey him!"

Who can this be? This is God in the flesh. God is manifested as a human being through the existence of Jesus Christ.

It is important to note that some of the apostles are fishermen and would have been acclimated to the water, storms, etc.

Jesus performed many miracles as they are stated throughout the Bible. There are 7 stated miracles performed by Jesus. The apostle John writes, that there would not be enough paper and ink existing in the world to document all the people Jesus helped and healed.

The following commentary is taken from Rediscover Jesus by Matthew Kelly pgs. 90 & 91:

Miracles are radical by their very nature, and so we shouldn't be surprised that they play a central role in Jesus' ministry. His miracles combined every aspect of his radical nature.

But in another sense, his miracles were ordinary. They were simple and practical, like his teachings. They were of real service to people, not just spectacular for the sake of being spectacular. They required no great effort; they were simply an extension of who Jesus was. They were never performed for show or out of any ego need.

Making the lame walk, giving sight to the blind, setting captives free – these were all radical. Forgiving people's sins – even more radical. And these were just everyday aspects of Jesus' life.

It is easy to fall into the trap of placing these miracles in a far-off place with people you never knew. But they are also here and now. It is a miracle that he forgives our sins even though he knows we will sin again. Would you forgive someone if you knew he or she was going to do it again?"

Mathew 9:35 Jesus went through all the towns and villages, teaching in their synagogues, preaching the gospel of the kingdom, and healing every disease and sickness.

CHAPTER 25

Most Translated Book

One book has been translated more than any other book throughout history. It stands out from all other books. The Holy Bible. The good book itself. It has survived despite many attempts to destroy it. It has always been under incredible scrutiny, yet it survives through each and every storm. Coincidence? I think not. God's word is always going to be with us. No matter what. It always will be. Even in our own English language the Bible has many, many versions. Though, I think the message is always the same. It is transcendent and is with us generation after generation. It is an ALL-TIME best seller. I am only a student of the Bible. I am a complete novice and quite inexperienced. I often oversimplify things and it is just one of my many, many faults. So, for me it comes down to both the Old and New Testaments. Jesus tells us He is the new covenant. Here comes my oversimplification: **God wanted His family back with Him.** Jesus paid the way and He paved the way for us to indeed be saved from our sin. Wow, what an incredible God that we indeed have. He loves us so very much. It is agape love. It is all the way. He is all in on each of us. The Bible does not claim to be either a science book or a history book. Yet, all of the science and history in the Bible is true and comes to pass. It does not get any better than the Bible being our life manual. I could give many, many illustrations but this particular chapter is about the versions and translations of the Bible. So here are a few examples though:

1. The Bible says the earth will be suspended in the air. While no person can explain gravity, the Bible clearly denotes the Earth's gravitational pull. We will not and do not fall off of the earth while it spins.

2. Israel will become a nation again, after not having a homeland for two thousand years. On May 14, 1948, Israel does become a nation again.

3. The prediction of the destruction of the Great Temple. This is where we get the expression, "no stone left unturned." This great structure would have been like a city within a city. It was grandiose. The walls were made out of 30 foot by 12-foot mortar blocks. It would have looked like a fortress. At first, the Apostles are doubtful, but as they realize Who is telling them these things God is telling them so then they want to know the who, what, where, when and why. So, in 70 AD, the son of Nero, Titus, comes into Jerusalem and destroys the Great temple. It takes six full months to systematically destroy the temple. It is still in ruins today.

4. The Old Testament speaks very specifically about circumcision. It instructs to wait seven full days, and then begin the procedure on a newborn male. I believe it was in the late 1930's, when it is discovered medically that it takes seven days for blood to build up to the point of coagulation as to promote proper healing and proper scabbing. God's instruction is always completely amazing. He always knows what is best for us, even if we do not know it ourselves.

I have many others, or should I say that He has many others. Suffice it to say that God does not need defending, and certainly does not need one of His servants to defend Him. He always exists right in your heart, if you are indeed looking for Him.

As far as we know, the Bible was written in Hebrew and then later transcribed into Greek, Aramaic, Latin and later into English and Spanish. It has survived wars and War Lords, burning and banishment, and even slander, insult, and ridicule. It is still with us and always will be. Jesus says, "My words will never fade away." The history of the Bible is so very compelling. Many have tried unsuccessfully to destroy it. Here is the thing though: it cannot and will not be destroyed. Many countries have tried to put an end to the good book but they have also been unsuccessful. Like our Jesus, the Bible lives on. It is a crystal-clear message of LOVE. I will move on to the versions:

One of the most often used versions of the Bible is the King James or the more modern New King James Bible. One of its most alluring qualities is its very clear word for word translation. It was first published in 1610 and became so popular in our 20th century that the New King James was introduced in 1982.

The Bible is indeed the most translated book ever. Once again, when you consider the context and the incredible journey the Bible has taken, it is certainly a divine miracle right from God.

The following statement is provided by ingcointernational.com

The Bible is a collection of ancient religious texts and is considered to be the word of God in both Christianity and Judaism.

The Bible is the most read and sold book in the history of the world, with an estimated sale amount of 100 million copies annually. It is not surprising that this text received the number 1 spot on this list. It has been translated into 469 languages.

Here are the many versions of the Hebrew Bible:

AMP Amplified Bible Word for Word plus amplification. Those looking for detailed meaning.

CEV Contemporary English Version Thought for thought Unchurched persons, easy to read.

ESV English Standard Version Word for Word. For readers of all ages.

GW God's Word Balance of word for word and thought for thought. Adults and children.

HCSB Holman Christian Standard Balance All ages

KJV King James Version Word for word Conservative and Protestant.

TM the Message Converts to modern American speech. Seeking fresh translation.

NAB New American Bible Word for Word. Catholic Audience.

NASB New American Standard Word form word. Conservative evangelical Protestant

NCV New Century Version Balance Highly readable in today's language.

NIV New International Version Balance Evangelical Christians.

NIRV New International Readers Balance. For Children

NKJV New King James Version Word for Word Readable version also for study.

NLT New Living Translation Balance Adults and Children.

NRSV New Revised Standard Version Balance Mainline and inter-confessional.

TNIV Today's New International Version Balance Readability without sacrificing accuracy.

When considering these Bibles, one also must consider these factors: context, writing tense, verse, mood, and observation. Tense could be present (current or continuous), perfect (ongoing results), imperfect (past but continuous), future (future but undefined), aorist (undefined, usually past).

Voice could be active, passive, or middle.

Mood could be indicative, imperative or subjunctive.

Observation would be focus and one word at a time.

The Bible encompasses all of these many versions and many translations. The Bible itself is a divine miracle. It is God's word spoken through man. The Bible is written by over 40 authors and there are 66 books to the Bible. One cannot stress enough both the simplicity and the relevance of the Bible. God's Word is just that. It is God's Word.

> **Ephesians 4:19 To know the love of Christ which passes knowledge; that you may be filled with all the fullness of God.**

Chapter 26

Route 66

There is a Route 66 and it certainly is somewhat famous. It was a highway completed in 1926 that connected the Midwest to the California coast. It stretched nearly 2,500 miles and basically went from the Chicago area to the Los Angeles area. It weaved its way through the Midwest then to the southwest and ultimately to the pacific coast. Only this is not the Route 66 to which I am referring. The reference is for the 66 books of the Bible. This is a map for our life, an instruction manual if you will. The message and messages that exist in the Bible are ones that I believe indeed are from God, and in fact exemplify the kind of person that God wants us to strive to be. We certainly have the very best teacher in Jesus. He teaches us by His love. It is a blessing among blessings that we have the Bible.

So what route will you take? Taking the route that the world suggests will ultimately lead to sorrow, destruction, pain and despair. The biggest problem is that of lack of hope. We need to understand and manifest the route which God wants us to take. It is a journey that truly is the road less travelled. Yet it is a road that God makes possible for us to follow.

The best part is what potentially waits for all of us at the end of this life journey; eternal hope, eternal life and an inconceivable eternal paradise. Once again that is the incredible love and incredible grace on display by our Lord.

So, we need to try to travel on Route 66 and let God lead us to where He wants us to be in every sense. His way is the right way and His course is the right course. Let us follow Him and He will indeed never lead us astray, but rather will lead us to paradise. The salvation of God is truly amazing. Consider the Bible. Consider the parables and what Jesus is teaching through them. Consider the beatitudes and the way God wants us to treat one another. Consider the Ten Commandments and the structure and attitude to live our lives. All of it is right there in our life manual, the Bible.

Ephesians 6:17 and the helmet of salvation, and the sword of the Spirit, which is the word of God.

CHAPTER 27

Mother Mary Knew

Mother Mary becomes a living prophet herself. In Luke chapter 1, Mother Mary declares that she will be blessed among all women. Our society deems Mother Mary as the blessed Mother.

Luke 1:46 (New Testament) the context of this by Mother Mary is quite amazing. She is 13 years old and visiting her cousin Elizabeth. She has not yet been visited by The Holy Spirit. She is not yet pregnant with Jesus, but the Angel has announced to her the coming of the Messiah and how God has favor on her. She writes that ALL generations will call her blessed. They surely do.

And Mary said: My soul magnifies the Lord. And my spirit has rejoiced in God my Savior. For He has regarded the lowly state of His maidservant: For behold, henceforth all generations will call me blessed. For He who is mighty has done great things for me. And holy is His name. And His mercy is on those who fear Him from generation to generation.

Mother Mary goes on to have several other children. She has four additional sons and two additional daughters. The daughters remain unnamed. The sons are James, Joses, Jude and Simon.

Mary was not without sin. She follows the guidance of Leviticus chapter 12. In making an offering to God.

This is the passage from Leviticus 12: 1 – 8.

Then the LORD spoke to Moses, saying, [2] "Speak to the children of Israel, saying: 'If a woman has conceived, and borne a male child, then she shall be unclean seven days; as in the days of her customary impurity she shall be unclean. [3] And on the eighth day the flesh of his foreskin shall be circumcised. [4] She shall then continue in the blood of *her* purification thirty-three days. She shall not touch any [b]hallowed thing, nor come into the sanctuary until the days of her purification are fulfilled.

[5] 'But if she bears a female child, then she shall be unclean two weeks, as in her customary impurity, and she shall continue in the blood of *her* purification sixty-six days.

[6] 'When the days of her purification are fulfilled, whether for a son or a daughter, she shall bring to the priest a lamb [c]of the first year as a burnt offering, and a young pigeon or a turtledove as a sin offering, to the door of the tabernacle of meeting. [7] Then he shall offer it before the LORD, and make [d]atonement for her. And she shall be clean from the flow of her blood. This *is* the law for her who has borne a male or a female.

[8] 'And if she is not able to bring a lamb, then she may bring two turtledoves or two young pigeons—one as a burnt offering and the other as a sin offering. So the priest shall make atonement for her, and she will be [e]clean.'"

Mary was undeniably blessed among all women. She delivered Jesus and then Jesus delivered Mary. She said herself I need a savior also. God has chosen Mary over all women. Generation after generation passes and the blessed Mother continues to be revered. She was present at the crucifixion of Jesus. Mary lived an additional eleven years. Mary dies in 41 AD.

Luke 1:26-28:in the sixth month the angel Gabriel was sent from God to a city of Galilee named Nazareth, to a virgin betrothed to a

man whose name was Joseph, of the house of David; and the virgin's name was Mary. And he came to her and said, "Hail, full of grace, the Lord is with you!"

CHAPTER 28

Messiah, Messiah, Messiah!

The word Messiah means anointed one or chosen one. This was someone with a special, God given, and God ordained purpose. Jesus fulfilled this prophecy. He was God as man. He is the Messiah. He saves all of mankind. By His stripes we are indeed healed; no other, but by His only. The Lamb of God is Jesus who takes away the sins of the world. That is the love of our Lord and savior. It is agape love. The only way to the Father is through the Son.

If Jesus Christ is not the Messiah than there is not a messiah. The timeline does not allow it. Again, if He is not, then there is not one. If you consider the place of His birth, the crucifixion and resurrection, His message of love and forgiveness in every circumstance, the preceding by John the Baptist, Bethlehem, Palm Sunday and the other well-known fulfilling of prophecies, He has to be the Messiah. Here is the thing though, He alone is the promised Messiah. He is sent from God the Father and He Himself is God the Son. He alone is the answer for our human sin. Once again, the incredible love of our God is evident in providing the savior. His purpose was to save us and that is exactly what He does. He saves all of us from our sin. He saves us from ourselves. It is an incredible blessing; one that should not be taken for granted.

Without Him we are stuck in our sin. Jesus is a gift from Heaven available to all who believe. He was lauded as He entered Jerusalem that first Palm Sunday as they chanted Messiah, Messiah, Messiah, yet five days later He would be tortured on a cross and killed. Three days later He would be resurrected. Now He belongs to us and we belong to Him for all eternity. He is our very best friend forever and ever.

He is the Messiah; Yours and mine for now and for always.

Acts 10:42 And He commanded us to preach to the people, and to testify that it is He who was ordained by God to be the judge of the living and the dead. To Him all the prophets witness that, through His name, whoever believes in Him will receive remission of sins.

CHAPTER 29

If I Could Touch His Coattails

I hate to think where any of us would be were it not for Jesus. I really do. To put it plain and simple; not a single one of us would even have a chance. Not a chance. Not even a glimmer of hope for salvation. Not even a glimmer. No, not even one. We are filthy wretches and that much is for certain. This is all about His grace. We do not deserve His grace, yet He gives it to us anyway. That is how much He loves us. I have come to the obvious realization that I am once again riding on the coat tails of Jesus. That is all that any of us are doing. He is all that I need, and He is all that I ever will need. He alone is all we need. You and I needed a savior. It is more than evident and obvious when you look at the world and when you look in the mirror. We have that savior in Jesus Christ. None is righteous. No, not even one. We are not holy, but He is holy. Why He loves me so, I will never even begin to understand and contemplate, but boy am I glad that He does. He really does, and He loves you just as much. It is all about grace. It is not something we deserve. It is not something that we do. It certainly is not something we earn. It is pure grace. The Bible is so very powerful, and the teachings of Jesus illustrate the how and the where that God wants us to be. If you remember the hemorrhaging woman from the Bible she thought if only I could touch His hem, then I will be cured. She did just that and was healed from that moment on. Her faith saved her and healed her, and it can do the very same thing for you. Let the love of our Savior work in your life. Jesus can and does do incredible things in a person's life. He manifests love consistently, completely and constantly. There is no love like His love. It is agape. It is indeed awesome. It always comes down to a choice. You can do it your way, or you can do it God's way. Invite Him into your life. It will make all of the difference. His way is always the best way. He knows us better than we know ourselves. Accept His gift and ride on those coat tails, as He invites you to eternity. He says abide in Me and I will abide in you. It is such a blessing. Understand that only through Him and Him alone are we saved.

> **Matthew 9:21 For she said to herself, "If only I should touch His garment I shall be made well." But Jesus turned around, and when He saw her He said, "Be of good cheer, daughter, your faith has made you well." And the woman was made well from that hour.**

CHAPTER 30

Thank You

Thank you. Does not really capture it at all. It is a nice sentiment, but I really do not think that thank you even begins to cover it. Not even close really. He died for each and every one of us so that our sin does not separate us from God. How do you thank someone for saving your life? Your eternal life. He saved me. He saved you. A wretch like me and He saved me any way. I will always wonder to myself why does He love me so much? I cannot answer that one but suffice it to say that He does indeed love me, and I feel it each and every day. I know that I do not deserve the salvation that He alone provides. When you have Jesus in your life you will always have hope. It is the hope of an eternity spent with Him in Heaven. Do you realize how much He loves you? It is downright enormous. He loves us so much that He went to the cross to take our sin away from us. He fulfills all of the scripture and all of the prophesy and He provides the way for us to gain eternal bliss in Heaven. God's love is without a doubt the greatest love that exists. So, we need to have an attitude of gratitude.

The Apostle Paul writes about faith, hope and love and he says the greatest of these is love. God's agape love is the greatest love you will ever experience. It is far beyond what we could ever imagine or even comprehend. What will you do with this tremendous gift? Will you accept it? So, we need to thank Him and say daily prayers of thanks for His goodness and His love. It is His glory and majesty which lead us to salvation.

> **Psalm 100:4 Enter into His gates with thanksgiving, and into His courts with praise. Be thankful to Him and Bless His name.**

CHAPTER 31

Amazing Grace

Grace is given as a tremendous gift to each of us. Grace cannot be earned. Grace cannot be bargained. Grace cannot be bartered. Grace cannot be assumed. Grace cannot be bought.

Grace can only be given by God himself. God provides the ultimate sacrifice through Jesus Christ. His (Jesus) sacrifice becomes our incredible grace.

The following is from Christianity.com

"Grace" is the most important concept in the Bible, Christianity, and the world. It is most clearly expressed in the promises of God revealed in Scripture and embodied in Jesus Christ.

Grace is the love of God shown to the unlovely; the peace of God given to the restless; the unmerited favor of God.

What is grace and what are some ways people have defined grace?

"Grace is free sovereign favor to the ill-deserving."(B.B. Warfield)

"Grace is love that cares and stoops and rescues."(John Stott)

"[Grace] is God reaching downward to people who are in rebellion against Him."(Jerry Bridges)

"Grace is unconditional love toward a person who does not deserve it." (Paul Zahl)

Grace is most needed and best understood in the midst of sin, suffering, and brokenness. We live in a world of earning, deserving, and merit, and these result in judgment. That is why everyone wants and needs grace. Judgment kills. Only grace makes alive.

A shorthand for what grace is - "mercy, not merit." Grace is the opposite of karma, which is all about getting what you deserve. Grace is getting what you don't deserve, and not getting what you do deserve. Christianity teaches that what we deserve is death with no hope of resurrection.

While everyone desperately needs it, grace is not about us. Grace is fundamentally a word about God: his un-coerced initiative and pervasive, extravagant demonstrations of care and favor. Michael Horton writes, "In grace, God gives nothing less than Himself. Grace, then, is not a third thing or substance mediating between God and sinners but is Jesus Christ in redeeming action."

Christians live every day by the grace of God. We receive forgiveness according to the riches of God's grace, and grace drives our sanctification. Paul tells us, "the grace of God has appeared, bringing salvation for all people, training us to renounce ungodliness and worldly passions, and to live self-controlled, upright, and godly lives" (Titus 2:11). Spiritual growth doesn't happen overnight; we "grow in the grace and knowledge of our Lord and Savior Jesus Christ" (2 Peter 2:18). Grace transforms our desires, motivations, and behavior.

In fact, God's grace grounds and empowers everything in the Christian life.

The English poet and clergyman John Newton writes the song "Amazing Grace" in 1779. Newton prior to his conversion to Christianity, is a slave tradesman by occupation. His faith turns him away from the slave trade and into the clergy. He writes the song and it becomes very popular even in his time. Today, it is still one of the most often used hymns in the Christian faith.

Amazing Grace Hymn

Amazing grace! How sweet the sound
That saved a wretch like me!
I once was lost, but now am found;
Was blind, but now I see.

'Twas grace that taught my heart to fear,
And grace my fears relieved;
How precious did that grace appear
The hour I first believed.

Through many dangers, toils and snares,
I have already come;
'Tis grace hath brought me safe thus far,
And grace will lead me home.

The Lord has promised good to me,
His word my hope secures;
He will my shield and portion be,
As long as life endures.

Yea, when this flesh and heart shall fail,

And mortal life shall cease,
I shall possess, within the veil,
A life of joy and peace.

The world shall soon dissolve like snow,
The sun refuse to shine;
But God, who called me here below,
Shall be forever mine.

When we've been there ten thousand years,
Bright shining as the sun,
We've no less days to sing God's praise
Than when we'd first begun.

God's grace is entirely amazing. Once again, it is not something that we earn, but is a gift that God bestows on each and every one of us. We have such an amazing God who gives such amazing grace.

> **Ephesians 2:8 For by grace you have been saved through faith, and not of yourselves; it is the gift of God, not of works, lest anyone should boast.**

CHAPTER 32

What About Right Now?

We seem to be a society of procrastinators. Satisfied to put things off until tomorrow. I will get to that is often our motto. Well, what about today or even this very moment. The question comes down to who do you love more? ... You or your God. We are all selfish at our base. It is so difficult because we are born into it, and we spend the majority of our lives trying to get ahead or trying to get that thing that will somehow make our lives more meaningful and worthwhile. News flash, you will always be left with emptiness with a focus on the material. The majority of the world does not know where it will get enough food to get through the day. We are blessed beyond belief. We take so very much for granted each day. This is in no way to suggest that God does not want you to have nice things and an abundance of blessings. He most certainly does. He just does not want you to lose sight of some very important things. First and foremost, the many blessings bestowed on us are His workings, not ours. Second, remember to worship Him, not some idol or tangible item, i.e. a car or house or job, etc. The bible says that all of these things will pass away. Indeed, all of those things will and do pass away. Jesus said all things will pass away but my words will never pass away. His words and this magnificent bible have survived generation after generation and century after century. There is a reason the bible is here yesterday, today and tomorrow. Matthew 24 says that only God knows the hour He is returning but don't you want to be prepared and ready? God's word survives all things, all peoples and all nations. This poor Jewish carpenter saved the world and saved you and me at the same time. He is simply awesome! We need to love Him, and each day live the day as we do love Him and manifest His ways into our lives. It is not easy but is surely possible if we let Him work. How does that one song go? ... Oh yeah, they will know we are Christians by our love ... By our love. It is not all that difficult when you think about it. After all, we have the greatest role model of all time in Jesus Christ. He loves us, and we need to return His love. Not tomorrow or next week or next year, but right now in this very moment. Do not put it off any longer cause the time is clearly at hand. So, live in Christ in the present and let tomorrow take care of itself. God says I made a covenant with you and you became mine. God is with you right now. Do you really want to make Him wait? ...... Him? Get busy doing things His way and stop doing them your way. His way is the greatest way.

> **Mathew 6:34 Therefore do not worry about tomorrow, for tomorrow will worry about its own things. Sufficient for the day *is* its own trouble.**

CHAPTER 33

The Greatest Event

It is the greatest event in history. Nothing else really is even close or could compare. What does it mean to you? The Resurrection of Jesus Christ is the single greatest event in history. It has changed the world as we know it forevermore and for all eternity. It alone is the greatest hope in all the world. No longer is there separation from God by our sinful nature. Rather, there is the ultimate substitution in Jesus (the new covenant) for our sins. He conquers our sin, whether past, present or future. He calls out from the cross "Tetelestai!" Which means it is finished. He has covered our sin for all time. It is paid for. God says I made a covenant with you and you became mine. Our relationship with God is made complete by the Resurrection. The only question that remains is what we will do with this outstanding gift that once again our God has provided. The answer lies within your heart. The apostle Thomas had a difficult time believing that Jesus rose from the dead. It is where we get the expression "doubting" Thomas. When he sees Jesus he says, "My Lord and my God." Jesus answers by saying Thomas you believe because you see. Blessed are those who don't see yet still believe. Do you believe? It is the true essence of faith. For us to rise, He needed to rise, and rise He did. God is so close to all of us. He is in our life every single day. We must invite Him in and TRY to be the person He wants us to be. Surely, we will all fall short of the glory of God. Yet, His love for us is enormous. It is agape. Easter is a new beginning for all of us sinners. What does it mean to you?

> **1 Corinthians 15:22 For as in Adam all die, even so in Christ all shall be made alive.**

Final Thoughts

The greatness of the Bible cannot be overstated. Biblical Canon is sound and thorough. The great prophesy of the Bible is astounding.

Do you have the capacity for God? Only you can answer that one. The answer lies within your heart. Your heart is where the existence of Christ is most profound. The heart is absolutely, positively, unequivocally and undeniably everything. It really is. It truly is. It is the most important thing to God. The very most important thing. Nothing else even comes close. It guides us through so much in life. It is what matters the most to God. It is indeed where we get the closest to Him. Without the heart we are so very far from God. He gives us the innate ability to indeed use our hearts. Using them in everyday situations and circumstances. Let my heart be open to You always Lord. He always uses His heart. The Bible says that wherein lies your treasure that your heart will be there also. If you contemplate that it is obviously true. It is definitely true. Ultimately, we feel all things with our heart. We do things with our heart. All things and everything. It comes down to what is the most important thing to you? Well, what is it? What is valuable to you? What is it that matters to you the most? What is important to you? Why is it important to you? Is it a person, a place or a thing, something material or tangible or is it God almighty? God knows our heart.

He made us. He knows everything about us. I mean everything. He knows our every desire. He knows our every want. He knows our every need. He knows our every intention. Wherein lies our heart? That is the biggest question of all for each and every one of us. The prayer should always be "Open the eyes of my heart Lord". Let me see as You see. Please keep my eyes open to Your ways. Then and only then can we really use that heart that God gave us. It is another one of his amazing gifts bestowed upon us. Please make me the very best person that I can become. Make me one of Your vessels. Make me an instrument of Your peace. Make me see things as You and only You see them. Use me for Your purpose and for Your goodness. Then and only then will I be truly blessed. Sometimes it will be when there is great turbulence, a storm or great trouble or tribulation in our lives. Do you turn to Him in those times? It takes incredible faith to indeed do so. Not just words, but the actions that accompany and follow that strong faith. If I can just be a little bit like Him I will be abundantly blessed, and I will be a blessing to others as well. I truly will. It will happen that way because that is God's way. It may not be such an easy thing, but that is how He wants us.

That should ultimately be our goal. To in fact bless others around you. I truly believe that we can bless others simply by the actions and examples of using our hearts. What better example could there ever be? There is nothing better than that. Absolutely nothing. You can be a wonderful role model without even trying to be one. Pretty amazing when you think about it. The heart can achieve things that the mind can only think about achieving. So, when it comes right down to it the heart will be the part of a person that matters the most. It will ultimately display our true character and it will reveal that character. It will display our courage sometimes even under the most difficult of circumstances. Open the eyes of my heart, Lord. Let God work in that heart. Using our hearts first in every situation will always be the correct path for us to indeed take. When my eyes are open I only become even more humble by this wonderful gift He has bestowed on all of us. It is agape love like no other. So, open those eyes and you will be amazed that your belief makes you see not the other way around. God's love is the greatest of all. Nothing compares to His love. What would Jesus do? Maybe a better question would be what would Jesus have me do? What would He have you do? So, let us open those eyes of our heart to all, and in all situations and all circumstances. It will make all of the difference in your life and in those whose lives you can affect. Use your heart all of the time for all time. We need to use our hearts each and every day. To this is how we should aspire. That should be how we spend our time. That should be our ultimate goal. God, our Father, should be lauded, praised for creating hearts within each of us that can be Christlike.

Praise the Lord .... I saw the light. Open your eyes, open your mind and open your heart, and invite Jesus inside. You will experience a peace like never before. A peace that seems almost impossible at first, but it is not impossible but rather it is downright amazing. The light is brighter than ever in these final days. Experience His love and His gift firsthand. Jesus is all about forgiveness. He covers all of the sin of the world for all time. He makes it so instead of God giving us the judgment we deserve, He gives us mercy instead. Feel the depth of His love and let His spirit guide you in your journey not only for the rest of your earthly life, but also for your eternal walk with Him in spiritual eternity for all time. His love for us goes on and on. It never ends. We may be limited by so many earthly things, but He does not know any limits. His love is limitless, and it fulfills every need, ever known and then some. He says I am the light of the world and whoever follows me will never be in darkness.

The light is brighter than ever in these final times. His love is agape love and is completely thorough. He proclaims from the cross, "Tetelestai!" (It is finished").

So, when you experience His light there is no turning back. Once He is in your heart He is there forever. You will never want to turn back and will soon realize and discover that what this world has to offer is simply artificial, temporal and not nearly enough and it is nowhere close to what God has in store for you. He is all consuming. He is all knowing. He is everywhere He is omnipresent and most of all He is right in your heart. He is the light of the world and He will be your beacon of hope. God loves you. He shows us the light. Praise the Lord. He loves you so very much. Praise Him and love Him. He certainly loves you.

The following excerpt is taken from Rediscover Jesus by Matthew Kelly pg. 118

"I have said it before, and I will say it again: Read the Gospels for fifteen minutes a day, every day. Allow the life and teachings of Jesus to sink their roots deep in your life. This will help you to get beyond your vague familiarity with the Gospels and develop a living, breathing, practical intimacy with them. If you make reading and reflecting on the Gospels a habit in your life, in time it will become a touchstone of inspiration and solace."

In conclusion, and I don't mean to oversimplify, but it really comes down to simple math. David and Isaiah (the writers of Psalms and Isaiah) could not have possibly known about crucifixion, and certainly could not have known Jesus. They are indeed amazing prophesies and you and I are given amazing grace. The more this is researched, the more prophesy is uncovered. All of this is history. It cannot be altered or argued. It happened. Maybe instead of history it should be called His/

Story. The Bible is God's ideation for His people who He loves so very dearly. The Bible is not provocative. The Bible is not news. The Bible is deliberate. Very deliberate. The Bible is TRUTH. The God honest truth. God says what He means, and He means what He says.

In summation, the most recurring theme in the Bible is love. God is great, and His Bible is great. Moreover, His Love is great. It is quite outstanding and astounding. Look how He adores us. His love is awesome. Completely agape love. GOD LOVES US!!

I would like to tell you, the reader, what the Bible is and what the Bible is not. I will start with what it is not. The Bible is not a fable, a fairy tale, mythology, fiction, conspiracy, falsity, and or a fallacy. The Bible is a miracle unto itself. The Bible is history, archaeology, honesty, prophecy, miraculous, sacred, and truth.

God does not care about your age, physical attributes, gender, color, socioeconomic status, political affiliation, creed, sexual orientation, education, race, last name, origination, language and or any other labeling demographic. He cares about your heart. God is not exclusive. God is inclusive. He loves each and every one of us.

The following paragraphs are from Rediscover Jesus by Matthew Kelly pg. 177:

When you stop, when you come to understand and deeply believe that this is only the beginning of our eternal walk with God our Father, everything is different. Different instantly, different forever. You are overwhelmed with the beautiful, deep, joyful and penetrating peace that comes from knowing that you are home today and forever. Fear is gone forever. You are like a ship that travels along a coast of endless safe harbors. Storms may come but the harbor is always moments away.

You have the one Captain, your Father, who is the Creator and Lover of all. He is not "like" a Father; he is your Father. He is more truly your Father than I can ever be. He is your Father. This is a defining difference which is the foundation of all that is true. Your faith and the saving grace of Christ is a game changer. Live in full sonship and daughtership and receive the fullness of His love and constant care for you. He is your real Father every moment and beyond all time.

Writing this has been a privilege and a blessing. I have learned so very much about the great Bible. If even one person is inspired by this book, then it is well worth it.

I am not making this up. This is not hypothetical. This is not fiction. This is not a hypothesis. This is not a theory. This is truth. The God honest truth. There is only one conclusion to come to and that is THE BIBLE IS GREAT!

> **Psalm 113: 3 From the rising of the sun to its going down**
>
> **The Lord's name is to be praised.**
>
> **Deuteronomy 31:8 The Lord himself goes before you and will be with you; he will never leave you nor forsake you.**

SOURCES

NKJV Holy Bible, Thomas Nelson Inc. New King James Version 1982
Rediscover Jesus Mathew Kelly, Cincinnati OH 2015
Wikipedia.org
Merriam-Webster.com
Bl.uk.com
oxforddictionaries.com
Bible history daily.com
Bible-history.com
Biblestudytools.com
Activechristianity.org
ingcointernational.com
Christianity.com

The Bible is great

The Bible is great! That may indeed be one of the very biggest understatements of all time. God has provided the life manual for us to obtain, maintain, and sustain spiritual life. The way we should treat each other with kindness, love, compassion and respect.

The Bible is great! It is the true, non-fictional account of the greatest book ever written. The good book has also endured many challenges and many critics. The Bible's history, archaeology and survival illustrate its divine authorship and compelling prophesy. So, take a ride on Route 66 it is indeed an adventure you will both need and enjoy. Jesus loves you and Jesus saves you.

God bless you

Printed in the United States
By Bookmasters